101 Essays to Empower You to Elevate Your Influence

Frank Agin

Founder & President
AmSpirit Business Connections

ISBN: 978-1-967521-14-2

Published by:
418 Press, A Division of Four Eighteen Enterprises LLC
Post Office Box 30724, Columbus, Ohio 43230-0724

101 Essays to
Empower You to
Build Momentum

Frank Agin
Founder & President
AmSpirit Business Connections

ISBN: 978-1-967521-08-1

Published by:
418 Press, A Division of Four Eighteen Enterprises LLC
Post Office Box 30724, Columbus, Ohio 43230-0724

Acknowledgement

In sincere appreciation
of Chase Agin.

You keep me in the loop
on all things sports and
are a great participant in
my Sunday test kitchen.

-3-
There Is No Shame In Asking

It's "human nature." People are hardwired to help one another. With this, the only thing that separates you from the help that you need is you asking. Dare to ask. Remember, if you are focused on giving and helping others, it is only fair that you also partake from the same process.

Let others know what kind of help you want.

Describe the types of people you are trying to meet.

Explain to your centers of influence how they can help you.

Solicit people for information that's relevant to helping you.

Understand this, if you are polite in asking of others and appreciative of whatever they give (even if it is only time), people will come through. Not everyone, but enough to make it all worthwhile. Equally important, however, when you reach out to others, you are in essence affirming that they have value to offer. It is a wonderful compliment. For that, they will be flattered.

-4-

A Star-Spangled Networking Adventure

Fact: Networking put Francis Scott Key in a unique position to write *The Star-Spangled Banner*.

During the War of 1812, the British detained a 65-year-old physician on their flagship. Immediately the elderly doctor's friends went to work trying to secure his release.

They had no direct connection to the federal government, so they networked through the doctor's patients. This led to a gentleman who happened to be the brother-in-law of Francis Scott Key, someone with prior experience as a United States District Attorney.

Key then worked through his contacts to connect with the President of the United States, James Madison, who allowed him to board the British flagship to negotiate under a flag of truce.

Before being released, however, Key and the doctor had to endure a night on the warship as it bombarded Fort McHenry. But the next morning, the American flag was still flying. And networking had put Francis Scott Key in a unique position to be inspired.

-5-
Questions Are the Answer

In his book, *Endless Referrals*, Bob Burg credits famous sales trainer J. Douglas Edwards with saying "Questions are the answer."

Burg goes on to elaborate that "The person who asks the questions controls the conversation. But when you ask the right questions, you lead the other person exactly in the direction you want to take them. So, you don't ever need to be pushy."

Questions are the answer. To make a positive impression at your first encounter with anyone, come with genuine curiosity to learn about them and an ability to formulate questions to facilitate that.

And as Burg points out in his book, you really never need to say anything. The only reason to make any statement is simply to set up the encounter for another question. Yes, questions are truly the answer for helping your new connection build a sense of "know you, like you, and trust you".

-6-
A Quick Payback

When it comes to professional networking and building those relationships, the mantra is simply "give to others and expect nothing in return." That, however, can be difficult. Life and business have ongoing pressures. After all, your mortgage payment won't wait for your good deeds to comeback to benefit you, right?

Nevertheless, you should never expect an immediate payback for your generous efforts. If, however, if you are looking for an activity that has a relatively rapid turnaround you should consider volunteering.

Giving of your time and talent to something you're passionate about will quickly provide you with a plethora of new contacts (mainly from other volunteers). Plus, volunteering offers you the ability to try new things, adding to your skillset. And study after study shows that by giving your time you become happier and healthier.

Each of these serves to immediately benefit you professionally, which provides a quick payback for your efforts.

-7-
LinkedIn Catch-Up Tip

There is no question that LinkedIn is a wonderful means of connecting yourself far and wide. If you're hesitant to use it because you feel woefully behind with relatively few connections, here's a tip: Join and participate in a LinkedIn group that represents a professional community of interest to you.

For the most part, these groups are highly welcoming and interested in new members. Once you've joined, you'll be one step closer to a plethora of like-minded business types. From here, you'll be able participate in conversations where you can learn and add value. From here, you'll be able to directly communicate with the group members, even if you're not yet "connected". From here, you can confidently send connection requests to people you might not otherwise know, as you have the group in common.

So, if you feel behind on your LinkedIn efforts, you can catch-up in a hurry. Simply find, join, and become involved with a group that is of interest to you.

-8-
Personalize, Personalize, Personalize

On a January 2020 episode of the *Networking Rx* podcast, author and speaker Bill Cates said, "In real estate, it's about location, location, location. When it comes to reaching out to new people it's about personalize, personalize, personalize."

Cates went on to elaborate that personalization is not simply inserting someone's name or company information into a merge file, then hitting a button to shoot out a canned e-mail or letter. Rather, personalization is about really gaining a sense as to who a person is and then incorporating what you've learned into one-on-one individualized communications.

There is no doubt that in the computer age, you can become extremely efficient in communicating with dozens, if not hundreds, of contacts with just a few keystrokes. However, as Cates implies, don't confuse efficient with effective. Personalization is not at all efficient, but it is highly effective in winning over the hearts and minds of your contacts. And in the end, that matters most.

-9-
Ubuntu

Ubuntu is a traditional African philosophy that explains how we are bound in each other's humanity. And it can be roughly translated as "I am because you are."

It embraces the idea that humans cannot exist in isolation. That we cannot be without each other and that you and everyone else depends on connection, community, and caring. Moreover, ubuntu instills the mindset that "When *you do* well, it spreads out. And the benefits to you are really for the whole of humanity. Everyone is better off."

With the ubuntu mentality, strive to put goodness into the world. When you see suffering or someone with an issue, look to help them, as helping one person really helps everybody, including yourself.

In addition, celebrate the victories of others. Remember, under the notion of ubuntu, another's achievements (not matter how small) somehow lift everyone, including you.

Remember, you are because we are.

-10-
The Leading Edge of Branding

If you're an entrepreneur, sales representative or professional, no doubt a business card is part of your daily attire. That is, you feel a sense of anxiety – just like when you forget your phone – when you don't have an ample supply of cards to share with that next prospective client or strategic business partner.

Your business card, however, is not just a functional component of doing business day in and day out. Done right, it's also an integral part of your corporate identity strategy. Most times, it's the first visual impression you make about your professional image.

For that reason, it's important that you invest in a business card design that represents your brand well. In addition, be sure to coordinate it with other aspects of your visual brand, such as letterhead, envelopes and brochures, as well as your website and social media.

Let your business card be the leading edge of your corporate identity.

-11-
Ben Franklin and the Internet

In her book, *The Networking Survival Guide*, social capital consultant Diane Darling shares that in 1727 Ben Franklin and other American patriots formed a sort of networking club for the purpose of mutual improvement. In fact, the group valued education so much that the members were instrumental in starting the University of Pennsylvania.

Darling queries, "Imagine what it would be like to meet each week with people of the caliber of Benjamin Franklin. The value of their intellect and viewpoints was so high that they wanted to learn from one another and share their knowledge."

Darling goes on to make the point that in the 21st century you are in a better position than Franklin and his network colleagues ever were. Think about it. The Internet opens up an entire world of great minds, information and resources to benefit from. You just need to be committed to exploring it and connecting with others.

-12-
Life Is Not Fair

No one ever said that life would be fair. Some people have more money. Others are taller. Some have super blue eyes. Still others seem to be in the right place at the right time. Life is "not fair."

However, as much as life is "not fair," it is "not unfair" either. That is, there is no great scheme to defraud you from getting your piece of the American dream or derail you from the goals you aspire to.

Understanding this, you should generally avoid the temptation to carry on as if somehow you have been cheated. You haven't. Moreover, this attitude is counterproductive. You see, few people can really identify with this "I have been wronged" attitude and even fewer people want to associate with those who believe this. And those who do, you don't really want to be around.

No, things are not perfectly equal. Accept that. And then move on. Everyone will respect you for it.

-13-
Networking Arithmetic

Simple math says if you subtract a larger number from a smaller one, you get a negative number. If you spend more money than you make, you go broke. Yet in networking, you give more than you expect to get and somehow that formula leads to prosperity. How can this be? Simple.

Much of what you give to others — referrals, information, and contacts — is not depleting you.

If you referred a job-hunting friend to an ace executive recruiter, what are you really out? Nothing, beyond a little time. To the two people you have connected, however, you have conveyed real value. And, in time, what will likely come back to you are things of significant value to you.

This is incredibly powerful stuff. The gist of this in networking terms is that what you give may not compare to what you get. It's not an exchange of like-kind items. For this reason, networking arithmetic doesn't follow conventional wisdom. So, you can't go broke by giving to others.

-14-
Polite Or Honest

Wharton School of Business Professor, Dr. Adam Grant shares that "When you're torn between being polite or being honest, err on the side of sincerity. It's better to be disliked but respected than to be liked but disrespected." Grant goes on to indicate that in the long run, the people we trust the most are those with the courage to tell the truth.

The reality is that the truth may sting, but, done right, the truth you share offers value. This is because your candor can really provide a path to improvement. Depending on the situation, it allows someone to be better or do better.

This does not mean that you should be brutally honest with your thoughts and opinions. After all, no one likes to feel injured. But there is that middle ground. You know: Where the feedback you share might not be complimentary but is constructive and well-intended in nature.

-15-
Be Welcoming

When you invite someone into your home, you go to great lengths to make them feel welcome. You try to make them feel comfortable and relaxed. You endeavor to create a standard of hospitality. You want them to want to come back. Moreover, you hope they share about their experience, so others know of your hospitality.

Obviously, you can't have everyone to your house. After all, much of the day you're not even there. So, while you can't invite everyone into your home, you can and do invite people into your presence.

Be welcoming to them to. Make them feel comfortable and relaxed. Exhibit a level of hospitality for being around you so they want to come back to visit. Create an experience that they share about with others.

If you consistently do this, you'll have no shortage of great people in your presence. And nothing but good can come from that.

-16-
Outside Your Niche-Driven Silo

To a degree, being successful requires that you dig into whatever you do and become a master of your craft. After all, we live in an increasingly specialized world where serving a niche well is imperative.

With that mindset, it can be easy to get holed up in a niche-driven silo - whether your office or another workplace - busily doing what you do. Serving clients. Wooing prospects. And learning how to become better at each of those things. Don't do the easy thing.

Yes, doing what you do will bring success. But that success will eventually plateau and begin to wane. Growth and lasting success come from outside your niche-driven silo. It's there where you'll meet wonderful new people and reconnect with colleagues and friends. It's there where you'll find groundbreaking new opportunities and fresh ideas.

Yes, dig into your craft and hunker down to serve your clients well. But remember to build into your week time to get out of your silo.

-17-
Don't Be Jealous

Best-selling author and personal development specialist Lewis Howes shared on Twitter, "Stop being jealous of people in their winning season. You don't know what they lost in their losing season."

Howes' tweet is impactful. It can be easy to become envious (almost jealous) of the achievements of others. Whether it's a promotion at work, accolades for a business or even a social media post that seems to have inexplicable popularity.

But you need to remind yourself that that those wonderful, notable moments never tell the full story. You might have forgotten about the failures or setbacks, if you knew of them at all. You're not privy to the heartache or seemingly endless toil that led to that one glorious instance.

As Howes implies, be happy for the victories of others. They've earned them. Moreover, it should serve as a beacon of hope that it's possible for you to achieve the same thing too.

-18-
Reward To a Grateful Brain

There is little question when you express your appreciation to someone, you make them feel good. But do you know who really benefits from this simple communication? You!

In October 2016, self-proclaimed neuroscience geek Melissa Hughes shared in an article entitled, *What Happens Inside A Grateful Brain?* that "A genuine expression of gratitude to someone else gives your brain a bigger reward than the person you thank!"

Hughes explained that when you make this expression of gratitude to someone, your body releases a neurotransmitter called oxytocin. This little mind drug makes you feel warm and fuzzy, as oxytocin is known to enhance your feelings of trust, empathy, and affection.

In short, when you go out of your way to tell someone that you really appreciate something about them or their effort, you're the one who benefits most. With that insight, drop whatever you're doing and find someone to thank. Your brain will give you a little something for the effort.

-19-
The Courage to Fail

In life, no one is undefeated. Every sports team has endured a loss. Every notable achiever can point to a disappointing stretch on the road to greatness. Every relationship, no matter how wonderful it might be, has endured a rocky patch or two.

Your life is no different. While you hope to have a career, business or life that continually trends upward, just like the stock market, occasionally you need to give back some gains.

When these moments hit, take solace in the fact that everyone has these moments. Everyone! So, don't be afraid to acknowledge your failings. Don't shy away from admitting that you could have done better.

In short, have the courage to fail. And do so with a degree of humility and a resolve to improve from the experience. In the end, this candor will draw others to you, making you more connected and better equipped to move forward on your journey of success.

-20-
I'm Possible

In Michael Maher's January 2020 *Weekly Words of Wisdom* Newsletter, the author and referral consultant shares: "You may think a situation is impossible, a person is impossible to deal with, or a goal too high. Remember the word itself says I'm Possible. A *simple apostrophe and space changes everything* and that is so true in life."

As Maher implies, there is no real "impossible," but just a mindset issue. A small tweak in thought and you're on your way to conquering what you might not have thought possible.

But it starts with you and your line of thinking. The situation, the person, the goal won't change until how you think about it does.

So, ask yourself, what could I do differently? How can I think about the situation differently? What are some things I have not considered? Who could I reach out to for some guidance?

In summary, as Maher challenges in his newsletter, "What will make your impossible, possible?"

-21-
How Do You Make This Better?

Here's a question. One you should have an answer for. Despite that, it's a question for which you'll always be looking for a solution. The question is this: "How do you make this better?"

What is the "this" you're trying to improve? It could be your job. It could be a business. It could be an organization. It could be a relationship. It could just be your life in general. How do you make it better?

There is an answer. Think on it. There is a way to improve things. There is. There always is. It might be something big. It might be something small. Whatever it is, find it. And then act. See through whatever you can to upgrade the situation.

Know this, however: No matter the improvement, there is still room to progress. Nothing is ever perfect. When you get to this point, again ask: How do I make this better?

-22-
Adding Value to Others

A great way of building relationships is giving to others. However, when people hear the term "giving to others," they tend to conjure up images of dragging out their wallets. That is not the case at all. In reality, giving to others is about adding value and you can do that in many different ways.

For example, you can do business with them, send them referrals, provide them useful information, spur them on, celebrate their successes, introduce them to strategic contacts or just lend a friendly ear.

Each of these things adds value. And when you add value to others, they cannot help but feel they know you, like you, and trust you. This builds the relationship.

And in addition, when you add value to them, somehow they are quietly compelled to return the deed at some point in time, likely when you need it most.

-23-
Three Ways to Handle Anger

Anger is very human. It's an emotion. So, becoming angry is not a failing. Not dealing with it is, however. Dr. John Schinnerer, host of *The Evolved Caveman* podcast, shares three simple tips for dealing with anger when you feel it rising up inside you.

One: Name it. Studies have shown that simply putting an emotional label on what you are feeling serves to reduce the intensity of that feeling.

Two: Identify what's underneath. Ask yourself, "What am I feeling beneath the anger?" Most times, there is an emotion preceding your anger, often on the heels of embarrassment, nervousness, sadness or hurt.

Three: Be appropriately assertive. Schinnerer shares that assertiveness lies midway on the scale between being a doormat and being aggressive. Assertiveness requires that you know what you need and speaking up.

The happiest and most successful relationships (personal or professional) involve those who can effectively deal with feelings of anger. Become one of those people.

-24-
Mirror, Mirror On The Wall

This is tough to do, but it is important if you want to succeed at, really, anything, but certainly in building relationships. What is it? Take a hard look at yourself and look for things to improve.

Sure, it is easy to look around and identify the shortcomings of others. But your success will come from fixing your own shortcomings. So, honestly answer questions like these.

How consistently do you conduct yourself in a confident, pleasant manner?

How much value do you really add to the world around you?

To what extent are you considered reliable by others?

Like the fabled magical mirror in Snow White, the answers you get in this self-examination may not be what you hoped for. But even if they're not, you now have some ideas as to how you can improve. And with this insight, you can commit to fixing your deficiencies which will greatly enhance your chances at success.

-25-
Who Are You

When you introduce yourself, it should obviously address the notion of "who you are." There is, however, no magic to stating this portion of a basic Introduction. After all, it is … well … basic. Nevertheless, this part of your introduction is important.

In this portion of your introduction, you need to clearly articulate your name. And it's best to lead with how you'd like to be addressed. For example, is it Mike or Michael … Kim or Kimberly? Then clearly state your title and the work you are associated with. Each of these is important.

Now, nothing says it has to be in this precise order … You could achieve the same thing by re-stating the example "Through my business, Breakthrough Champion, I help service-based businesses get more referrals … I am Matt Ward" Or "I am with Breakthrough Champion. My name is Matt Ward and I help service-based businesses get more referrals."

While there is no magic, be prepared to clearly state "who you are."

-26-
Who's Holding Your Ladder?

Dr. Rob Bell, sports psychologist, podcast host and professional speaker, shared that in 2014, when Kelvin Sampson became the head basketball coach at The University of Houston, his former boss at the University of Oklahoma sent him a ladder. That's right ... a ladder.

The gift to Sampson, who had a distinguished coaching resume, was symbolic.

It symbolized all the people whose hands had been on that ladder to put him in a position for success. Those included not just players, but also other assistants, managers, wives, alumni, and administrators. They all contributed.

The symbolism was not lost on Sampson. He stood on that ladder when this team cut down the nets after Houston won its first conference championship in 27 years.

Who's holding your ladder? Who's contributing to your success? Be sure to take a moment to acknowledge them.

-27-
The Thin Edge of the Wedge

You've got big dreams. No matter who you are or where you are, you're aspiring to something more than what you have now. It's simply human nature to want for something more.

At times, however, that ambition can seem so big that it's daunting; so huge that it's impossible to start. Don't be deterred. Simply ask yourself, what's the thin edge of the wedge.

This idiom refers to a time before equipment and machinery when people used wedges to move seemingly immovable objects. If they could just get the narrowest side of a wedge into a gap, that would allow them to do bigger things, in time.

So, what's that one small, minor action to get you started on realizing your dreams? Act on that. Then look to do something a fraction larger. And then again. And again. Eventually your aspirations are realized. And it all started with the thin edge of the wedge.

-28-
A Perfect Shame

In 1959, Pittsburgh Pirates pitcher Harvey Haddix faced off against the Milwaukee Braves, winners of the last two National League pennants. Haddix was fearless in his approach, downing the first three batters in the first inning and not given up a run, walk, or hit.

Then, he did it again in the second inning. Then, the third. The fourth. Fifth. Sixth. And so on. In a perfect game this continues for nine innings. After 11 innings, Haddix still had no blemishes on his effort.

Unfortunately, the game went to a 12th inning. The Braves scored a run, winning the game. Sadly, rather than having a perfect game on his record, Haddix was credited with a disappointing loss. Despite this, his effort is referred to as the greatest game ever pitched.

The lesson is this: Don't be hemmed in by the standards of others. Whatever your work is, do your very best, and know that it can be characterized as great, even if the result is not exactly what others hoped for.

Frank Agin

-29-
Last Letter; Last Word Exercise

On the *How To Be Mesmerizing* podcast, host, author and thought leading psychologist Tim Shurr shares a fun, but very effective exercise for improving your listening skills. Shurr encourages you to listen for the last word your conversation partner utters when you're at an event or even casually chatting with family and friends. Simple, right?

Then your next question or comment needs to start with the last letter of the last word spoken. Now, as an example, the person says, "Every day, I go for long walk with my dog." Given the last word is "dog," your response should start with the letter G. Get it? Then you might say, "Good for you. Where do you go for these walks?

So, doing this makes you to pay attention, listen and learn. Now, if you replay this piece, you'll find that this program follows Shurr's exercise. Every sentence starts with the last letter of the last word of the previous one. Excellent, huh?

-30-
Character Over Reputation

Famed basketball coach, John Wooden once shared, "Be more concerned with your character than your reputation. Character is what you really are. Reputation is what people say you are."

Wooden's words are insightful. Your reputation is never truly accurate. It's based on tiny moments of your life over time. These small snapshots or sound bites are only notable moments that others have chosen to seize upon as being important based on their limited perspective of you.

Your character, however, is true. It's what you are. It's who you are. It's not a simple portrayal of some fleeting instant where facts and circumstances are limited. It's what permeates your thoughts and actions even when no one is there to witness it. It beats in your heart 24 hours a day.

Yes, focus on character over reputation, as character is what you are. And not just what others think. If you do this, in time your reputation will closely align with your character.

-31-
Commit To Daily Action

You want a productive network. You know you do. One that keeps you flush with people you can turn to for great referrals, insightful information, and additional priceless contacts.

You want this. Everyone does. How do get such a productive network? Simple. Make it a priority to share great referrals, insightful information, and priceless contacts.

It's no secret. To get things out of your network, you first need to build those same things in your network. When you contribute to others – family, friends, colleagues, clients and even people you hardly know – you build those relationships. And you set in motion amongst your network a powerful desire to contribute to you in return.

So, every day commit to doing something to contribute to your network, as each action is a step towards building the network you want. What are you doing today to build your network?

-32-
Building Authority Via Weakness

As Brian Ahearn reminds us in his book *Influence People*, "Studies show people are more likely to comply with a request when it comes from an expert."

While that's insightful, it likely begs the question, "How can I make this influence tactic work for me?" Well, Ahearn offers insight for that too. He shares, "Studies show you can increase your trustworthiness – and in turn your authority – simply by admitting a weakness early on. Then, be sure to share your strengths immediately afterwards." According to Ahearn, this approach will ensure that people remember your strengths more than your weaknesses.

So, to ensure you have a lasting impact with your message, say something like, "No, I don't know anything about the political implications. But I've spent a year studying the financial implications. This pays for itself in a year or less."

As Ahearn reminds, your authority is built through your weaknesses and then on to your strengths.

-33-
Expressing Admiration

Think of the last person you spoke to. What qualities about them do you admire? Did you somehow convey that sentiment to them? Why not?

Now think about this. When you discover that someone admires qualities you possess, do you tend to have a heightened degree of admiration for them? I bet you do.

So, it stands to reason that a super simple, highly effective and very inexpensive means of drawing others to you is to let them know what you sincerely appreciate about them. You only need a moment to say it. Or a few keystrokes to fire out an e-mail. Or a postage stamp and a little ink on a handwritten note.

With this little bit of effort, you set in motion powerful forces that serve to amplify your relationship with whomever you choose.

So, what's stopping you? It's easy to do. And the rewards are amazing. So, let someone know why you appreciate them.

-34-
Paperclip To House

In the summer of 2005, Kyle MacDonald shared on the Internet that he was attempting to own a house by trading up from his starting position –a red paper clip. Immediately he traded the paper clip for a fish-shaped pen.

Another person saw more value in the pen than in the handmade doorknob he had. And similar logic followed as the doorknob was exchanged for a camp stove, followed by a 100-watt generator, then a Budweiser sign, which ultimately garnered a snowmobile.

From here, MacDonald secured an afternoon with rock star Alice Cooper, which he traded for a KISS snow globe, which converted into a paid movie role. Finally, someone offered a farmhouse in exchange for the movie role.

This is a wonderful metaphor for networking. The things you offer up to your network have more value in the hands of others. And what you get in return has a whole lot more value to you. In short, networking arithmetic is a whole different breed of math.

-35-
The Personal Care Package

In his popular book, *MORE … Word of Mouth Referrals, Lifelong Customers and Raving Fans*, professional speaker Matt Ward introduces the concept of the Personal Care Package as a means of really staying on the radar of your best referral sources.

He shares, "To cut through the noise of marketing and advertising that bombards your contacts every day, you must find some very clever ways to reach them. Developing your personal care package is the key. This is a series of things you do to ensure that you remain on the top of your contact's mind."

Ward essentially asks, "What is it that you could send to your best referral sources?" And he shares that it has to show that you've taken note of who they are, what they've said, or what really matters to them.

Maybe it's a unique trinket … an article or other information … or maybe chocolate-covered bacon. Figure that out and then take action.

-36-
Add Value Via Social Media

An effective use of social media is to share with your online network. Sure, you can enlighten others on who you are, who you're with and what you're doing. But beyond just being like your own personal publicist, you can use social media to add value.

Adding value is important whether you're networking in a traditional manner or online. People simply want to associate with those that have something to offer. It is human nature. So, you can provide significant value to your online network by sharing content. This can include offering information, providing insights, or simply alerting others to opportunities.

Furthermore, just like contributing content, you can add value by engaging your network. Ask questions that allow others to share. Solicit feedback, allowing others to chime in with an opinion. Create a forum for discussion and debate. Each of these creates interaction. With you. Amongst others. And all of it creates value within your network.

-37-
Getting Involved

To be successful in any business or profession, you cannot just hole-up in front of your computer and work the phone. You need to shower up, brush your teeth, and get out amongst people. Find groups and organizations to join.

Know this, however, you cannot just belong. You cannot just be in the community. You cannot just be in the Chamber. You cannot just be part of the Church. You cannot just belong.

To develop strong relationships – you know, build know, like, and trust – you must get involved. Roll up your sleeves (actually or figuratively) and lend a hand. Be an officer in a group. Be a committee member of an organization. Be something (anything) more than just a name on a membership roster.

By doing so, you raise your level of exposure. And you demonstrate your level of commitment to something more than just you. When you do these things, others will not be able to help but know, like, and trust you.

-38-
Network Like a Boy Scout

In his book *Who Do You Need To Meet*, professional speaker Rob Thomas reveals that achieving his Boy Scout Eagle Badge taught him the value of community, relationships and service.

He shares, "That training inspired me to become a civic-minded adult. I discovered that if my goal is to meet more people and have them know me better, the easiest way is to volunteer and really become involved."

Thomas continues to make the point that when you come out of your corner of the world to volunteer, you find yourself shoulder to shoulder with people who share your passion for something. Likewise, they've also come out of their corner of the world to serve too.

So, if you want a "feel good" way to get yourself networked, find a charity, organization, or initiative you're passionate about. Then offer up your time, talent and conviction to make a difference. As Thomas might term it, network like a boy scout.

-39-
Winning The Blame Game

Humans are hard wired for self-preservation. That is, you're geared to steer clear of potential dangers and protect yourself at all costs. In many respects, this is a good thing. It's largely kept mankind safe and thriving for literally eons.

This is good, but beware. Sometimes that instinct can undermine your relationships. How? When things in your life don't work out, that impulse to safeguard yourself can lead you to blame others for the misfortunes you encounter.

No doubt, other will wrong you or simply makes mistakes. But before you lash out (whether inward or outward), think through the situation. What could you have done differently to avoid it?

No, this does not excuse a mistake or misdeed, but it allows you to get a grip on your emotions. This will help you move forward in a mature, professional manner. And that will ensure you continue to win people over in your relationships.

-40-
Get First Sometimes

If you're a student of networking, then you've likely heard the Golden Rule. If not, here goes: The Golden Rule of Networking says, "Give First, Get Second." In a nutshell, those who are highly proficient at building relationships know that they need to do things for other people and then simply trust that good things will come back to them at some point in time.

From time to time, however, someone you've never done anything for does something for you. That's okay. The Universe is not out of whack. It's likely that all your prior "giving" efforts have made their way back to you. In essence, fate has simply shined on you.

Graciously thank them for what they have done. Then make an effort to learn how you can add value to them. And finally make a mental note to keep your eyes and ears open for opportunities to serve them.

-41-
Crafting Note Card Commercials

In her *Networking Ninja* series on YouTube, body language expert Alison Henderson encourages you to use note cards to craft various impactful 30-second commercials. According to Henderson, on individual cards you should draft short sentences that address a variety of topics like:

What you do?
Who you do it with?
Short client stories.
Insightful tips.
Things that differentiate you.

Then leading up to a networking activity, pull out the sequence of cards that make the most sense based on the circumstances of the event. This gives you a fresh, unique and appropriate introduction.

From here, take the time to practice. As Henderson indicates, work through your cards. Read them when you have time between meetings. Recite your commercial aloud as you get ready in the morning and during your commute to and from work. With this note card preparation and practice, you'll make a lasting impact with your introduction at any event.

-42-
Networking TQM

In his book *Achieving Success Through Social Capital*, Dr. Wayne Baker relates a means of improving your networking skills using a manufacturing industry practice known as Total Quality Management, or TQM. The first step is to list out things you're not doing that you should be, like:

- Not appropriately thanking someone; or,
- Not promptly returning a telephone call or e-mail; or
- Failing to actively listen when engaged in conversation.

And this list could go on. Once you have the list, make a tally by each defect when you fail to do what you should have.

After several weeks, you'll gain a sense as to what you can improve. But as Baker points out, just knowing that you're tracking certain behaviors will serve to help you avoid committing these failures, which creates improvement in and of itself.

In short, through networking TQM you'll improve your networking PDQ – pretty darn quick.

-43-
Can I Put You On Hold?

Who likes to be put on hold? No one. People hate being put on hold. Who likes to hear, "I can't talk right now. I'll get back to you ASAP"? Again, nobody like this.

Now if you operate in the real world (and you likely do), you know that putting someone on hold or having to call them back is inevitable, right? It can be a good problem, as at times things are coming at you so fast you need to use these tactics to keep a handle on things.

Knowing that people generally do not like these ploys, use them sparingly. When you do have to use them, make the hold time brief and the call back time quick. And if for whatever reason you can't, get with the person immediately to re-frame their expectations.

No one like to be put off. But people cannot help but like someone who respects that.

-44-
Leading From the Bench

In his book *The Next One Up Mindset*, mental edge guru Grant Parr shares a quote from Abby Wambach, the longtime superstar forward for the US Women's National Soccer Team.

Wambach said, "If you're not going to be a leader on the bench, how can you be a leader on the field."

Parr goes on to elaborate, that whomever you are and no matter what your role, lead. Don't wait to be anointed as the team's star. Don't wait to be elected team captain.

It's important to note that this notion has application beyond athletic competition. It's also sage advice for corporate America, entrepreneurial realms and even those associated with non-profits and social initiatives. It applies to really anyone who has interaction with others.

Whomever you are. Whatever you do. Embrace your role. Take pride in it. Lead others by how you carry yourself and support others. No matter the endeavor this will get you off the figurative bench that much sooner.

-45-
Wanted ... Strangers

Good old Mom told you not to talk to strangers. And that was good advice. Unfortunately, society has that fringe of individuals looking to prey on the innocence of youth.

But that was then. This is now. And you're no looking that little kid, are you? No! You live in the grown-up world. And while you still need to be aware of certain individuals, generally speaking you're good to talk with strangers.

After all, in the grown-up world strangers are people just like you. Decent. Responsible. And aspiring, to list a few attributes. In summary, these strangers are new contacts that have a wonderful knack of becoming good friends, great clients and gateways to incredible opportunities.

So, it's now okay. You can forget Mom's warnings. Get out there and talk to strangers. But do remember to eat your vegetables. They're still good for you.

-46-
Harvard Beats Yale 29-29

In 1969, The Yale Bulldogs were ranked as one of the top football teams in the Associated Press polls. Moreover, the media considered them as the team to easily win the Ivy League conference. None of this was surprising, as football experts considered them to have a litany of stars and professional prospects on their roster.

When this Ivy League juggernaut was to play its rival on November 23, sports writers and analysts all proclaimed that Harvard did not stand a chance. The media's general consensus was that the Crimson lacked talent at key positions and had no standouts or star players.

Despite the media propaganda, Harvard overcame a 16-point deficit late in the game to earn a 29-29 tie. In so doing, Harvard shared the Ivy league title with much-touted Yale.

The lesson is that you shouldn't buy into the hype of others. Experts can say whatever they want. The reality is that you get the final say.

-47-
A Favorite Four-Letter Word

On her *Facilitator on Fire* blog, Kay Coughlin (an expert on connecting across generations and genders) proclaims that her very favorite four-letter word begins with "F." No, it's not that word. It's "fail."

Why? She explains, "It's simple, really. When we fail, we learn. When we learn, we grow. When we grow, we have a much better chance at succeeding – as long as we keep going."

Coughlin goes on to explain that failure is normal. It's natural. And she proclaims it to be a learning tool and not weapon to use against yourself or that others should use against you. Failing is not a bad thing. Not unless you allow it to be.

She chides the conventional wisdom that "if you fail, you'll never succeed." Rather she makes a counterpoint: Without failure you can't possibly ever succeed.

Coughlin is right. Fail! And do so often. Learn from it, sure. Embrace it, absolutely. But whatever the case, make it your favorite four-letter word, too.

-48-
Become the Person

The key to successful networking is getting great people interested in you. This, however, raises the question, "How do I get people interested in me?"

The best way to answer that is to ask yourself this, "Why do I want to associate with certain people?" After all, it only makes sense that the reasons why you want to associate with certain people are likely the same reasons why others would want to associate with you.

With that simple revelation, if you adopt the same characteristics, attitudes and habits of the people you want to network with, then others will want to network with you.

So, take the time to get at the answers to these three questions:

What do you want to KNOW about others?
What makes you LIKE others?
What builds your TRUST in those people?
With these answers, adopt these characteristics in a genuine way.

In very simple terms, you need to *become the person you want to network with.*

-49-
Who Knows Who

Your network is an asset, just like a bank account or a house. Perhaps not value you can spend tomorrow, but value, nevertheless. After all, it's your network that helped build your business, get that promotion and find information to make smart financial decisions.

So, your network has value. And it's important that you not only understand that, but that you undertake an assessment of that value. One way you can generally assess the value of your network is by examining its interconnectedness.

Ask yourself: To what extent do the people I know, know each other? Do they pretty much all know each other or are they relatively unconnected to one another? If the people you know all know each other, your network has less value than if your network is a collection of people with a loose affiliation to one another.

Whatever the answer, you now have the insight to go about improving the value of your network.

-50-
The Antithesis of the Hard Sell

In his book, *Endless Referrals*, hall of fame speaker Bob Burg refers to "hard selling as the antithesis of networking." Logically then, the exact opposite of the hard sell is networking.

When you sell, you look to execute a fair exchange of what you have to offer for the hard-earned money of another. As Burg implies, when you push too hard for that exchange, you serve to violate the trust they have in you. This repels them from you.

When you network, however, you serve others. And that naturally builds trust. And that trust draws people to you.

Here's the reality: People enjoy buying! In fact, many really love to shop. However, no one likes to be sold.

So, the best way of advancing yourself is to put yourself out there in the service of others. With that, they will want to know what you're about and what you have to offer. In time, they will enjoy buying from you.

-51-
Networking 'To Do' List

According to Marlene Wilson's *Survival Skills For Managers,* "The way you ensure that you keep moving towards your goals and objectives...is to keep a daily 'to do' list."

With that, what networking activity is on your 'to do' list? Every day make sure that you include something that further networks you. It can be as simple as following up with just one client, prospect, or old friend, just to touch base.

Or your list might have something that's a little more involved, such as: Send an article or website link to someone who might value the content. Or make a point of liking, commenting on and sharing a couple social media posts. Or, introducing two people that don't know each other. Or, attending an event and committing to meet two new people.

Whatever the case, having a networking 'to do' list will ensure that you keep this success-building habit top of mind, which will move you towards your goals and objectives.

-52-
What Can't You Do?

Sir Roger Bannister, neurologist and British middle-distance runner who ran the first sub-4-minute mile in the early 1950s once remarked, "The human spirit is indomitable. No one can ever say you must not run faster than this or jump higher than that. There will never be a time when the human spirit will not be able to better existing records."

Think about that. No one believed that humans could run a mile in under four minutes. That is, until someone did. No one believed that we could safely sail beyond the horizon. That is, until someone did. No one believed that we could fly in the sky, walk on the moon, conquer disease and countless other accomplishments. That is, until someone did.

Given that track record, what can't you do? Do the thoughts and theories of others limit you? No! Of course not. Only you can limit you. So, become committed and get busy.

-53-
Become a Capitalizer

In a newsletter entitled *Positive Psychology Tools with the Biggest Bang for Your Buck,* executive coach and relationship expert Dr. John Schinnerer shared that, according to Shelly Gable of the University of California, Santa Barbara, "one of the keys to transforming good relationships into great ones is to learn the skill of capitalizing on the good news of others."

Gable goes on to say that "The best response to the good news of others is to feed off their excitement, ask questions and show genuine interest, creating a positive upward spiral."

Look around. Someone you know has accomplished something wonderful. And others might have more moderate achievements. Whatever the case, good news abounds. Celebrate it.

Send them a short-handwritten note. Take time from your day to call. Get up out of your chair and walk down to theirs to pat them on the back. Cheerfully share the accolades on social media.

No, none of these changes the world. But it sure can make someone's day.

-54-
Paint a Picture

If you're looking to get referrals, know this: No matter how much someone might like you, they don't magically know how to refer you. If you want referrals, it's your job to get your network primed to recognize who is a good candidate or what might be an opportune situation. To build this recognition in the minds of those you look to for referrals, do these two things:

One, develop a series of short statements that concisely convey what you are looking for. Make these short and simple (so simple that a 5th grader could understand them). And,

Two, in these statements, don't just give basic facts. Facts alone are generally not memorable. Rather build these facts within a compelling story, example or analogy. This will make what you have to say enthralling.

If you do these two things, you will serve to paint a picture in the minds of others as to what a good referral opportunity looks like.

-55-
Chase Just One Rabbit

Your network is built one relationship at a time. So, as you are out at events, don't feel the need to race about meeting as many people as possible ... having quick, shallow conversations ... collecting business cards and then haphazardly following up with a plethora of people you can hardly remember.

Rather work to have involved conversations with just a few people, and then attend another gathering and do the same. Learn about people. Invest time in who they are. Be genuinely interested. Conduct yourself so that when you follow up, you can do so with substance.

Heed the old Indian proverb that says, "An eagle that chases two rabbits, catches none." This is true of relationships as well. You won't be able to develop lasting 'know, like, and trust' if you are focused on multiple relationships at any one time.

Have the presence of mind to chase just one rabbit at a time.

-56-
Small Talk to Happiness

In one of her recent weekly *Neuro Nugget* newsletters, neuroscience geek Melissa Hughes shared that "People who stop for a conversation with their barista are happier than those who grab their java and rush out."

She went on to explain that studies show that small talk or even just making eye contact or exchanging a smile can boost your mood and make you feel more socially connected.

Hughes will be the first to say that this is not limited to Starbucks or the local place you get your favorite cup of joe. It'll work at the grocery store checkout. At the dry cleaner. With the mail carrier. You can give yourself this little mood boost anytime you make eye contact, smile, and say hello.

So, take her challenge today. Engage in a little small talk with anyone you can, stranger or friend. See how it makes you feel.

-57-
Finish With a Strong Ask

If you want referrals, you can't just ask for them. You must be clear as to what you're looking for and you must finish with a strong "ask".

For example, when you say, "A good referral for me is someone in transition or not happy with the direction of their career." it leaves others wanting to say, "OK, that's nice." Your "ask" is wimpy; in fact, you didn't really "ask" for anything.

A strong ask, however, has all the same information, but injects a call to action. Like this: "If you know of someone in transition or not happy with the direction of their career, please introduce me to them."

That strong "ask" (...*please introduce me to them*) makes a subtle, but important command to your referral partner. It says, "If you see or know of this, please send it my way ... Or give me their number ... Or invite them to my seminar."

When seeking referrals, finish with a strong ask.

-58-
Be Victorious in Defeat

Life is not an endless succession of forward progress. Eventually you will endure a setback. When you do, you must fight through any discontentment and not allow it to affect those around you. To do this, remember these four things:

One, put the setback or disappointment in perspective. Just how vital is it compared to your entire life? It's likely relatively small.

Two, remind yourself that the setback does not define you. And it does not undo your prior accomplishments.

Three, remind yourself that your failure is not fatal. Rather it is just a temporary setback.

Finally, with every setback, you gained something. You need to take an inventory of what that is and use it to move forward.

By working through each of these thoughts in the face of a setback or disappointment, you will hold yourself a little taller and prouder, improving how others see you.

-59-
Cultural Impact

In a February 2020 post on Twitter, social scientist Adam Grant of the Wharton School of Business shared this insight: "Before taking a job offer, it's worth asking, 'Do I want to become more like the people here?' You can aspire to change the culture of a group, but don't overlook how the culture will change you. Few of us are immune to the values of the people around us."

Grant's tweet is worth taking to heart. Even if you're not contemplating a new position or job change, you need to ponder for a moment the impact your network has on you. Collectively, it either raises you up or pulls you back in one way or another. Even, individuals within your network also either raise you up or pull you back.

Yes, absolutely serve your network. But look for your network to serve you, too. So, do what you can to increase your interaction with those in your network who help raise you up.

-60-
Lean Into Change

John Shook, an organizational change expert who helped bring *lean management* to the United States from Japan, once remarked, "It's easier to act your way to a new way of thinking than think your way to a new way of acting."

Shook's insightful thought has had an impressive impact on corporate America, creating innovation, growth and opportunity across a variety of industries. But this notion that action is the best catalyst for improved thinking has broad application to your life as well.

Start eating healthier and you'll come to believe in its positive impact on you. Commit to learning and you'll soon believe in the importance of knowledge. Focus on being more respectful and you'll quickly believe that it's the foundation of solid relationships.

The most effective way to change what you think and believe is to first change what you do. So, if you want to change how you think about anything, lean into a new way of acting.

-61-
Contagious Generosity

In their book *Connected*, university professors Nicholas Christakis and James Fowler related research that demonstrated that good deeds inspire more of the same.

They placed 120 students in groups of four to participate in a capitalistic exercise where some would profit, and others would lose. Each student was given a sum of money and had the option of giving some funds to others at their own expense.

The exercise was repeated, with different group configurations. In the first few rounds, no money was gifted.

However, unbeknownst to the participants, one student was a confederate -- someone who was in on the experiment. At one point, this confederate started to give away some of his money to others.

In the exercises that followed, the people who benefited from the gift gave more. Even those who only witnessed the gifting began giving more. Generosity continued to spread.

The lesson: People don't just give; they're somehow moved and inspired to do so. Take it upon yourself to be the inspiration.

-62-
Communicate LUV

Tim Shurr, host of the *How To Be Mesmerizing Podcast* encourages his listeners, as well as his corporate coaching clients, to communicate with love. Except that the love that Shurr talks about is not L-O-V-E love, but rather L-U-V love.

Shurr's LUV is an acronym reminding you to Listen to Understand and Validate. He goes on to explain that the best communicators do more listening than talking. But it's more than just listening. No, the listening that Shurr speaks to goes deeper.

Before they share anything, great communicators listen to not only understand the other person's point of view, but also to gain a sense as to how the other person feels about the situation. And if neither of those are clear, they will ask questions to gain further clarification rather than making assumptions about what the person might have meant.

As Shurr implies, the best communication involves caring. And the most effective caring is simply LUV. Listen to understand and validate.

-63-
A Good Laugh

There is no such thing as a bad laugh. Think about it. Never has even a mild chuckle left anyone in a worse position. No, laughter serves to lighten any mood and lift any spirit, even if just for a moment.

Laughter, which is the productive result of humor, is the universal language. Everyone appreciates laughing. And thus, any laugh is a good one.

With that, take time every day to find something to laugh about. Read the newspaper funnies. Ask your Alexa device to share a joke. Look to Facebook, Instagram, or Twitter for something amusing.

Whatever it is, take it in and laugh. Forget your troubles, even if just for a minute. Don't hold back that smile. Let the comedy of the moment warm your soul.

And then take an extra second to share your good spirit with another. That goodness will then ripple forward in time. And it all started with a simple laugh.

-64-
Fraught With Challenges

Life is fraught with issues and challenges and it's often a heavy burden to move forward. Fortunately, the answers lie somewhere neatly embedded in your network. You just need to tap into it.

Start by making a list of the issues and challenges that you face. Then, make a list of those in your network you can reach out to for ideas, insights, connections, and opportunity. Think of all the people you know: friends and family, colleagues and co-workers, customers and clients, employees and vendors, as well as neighbors and community contacts. It's truly a treasure trove of resources and solutions.

Then, stop for a moment. Before you reach out, take a little more time to detail all the ways you can help these people. What ideas, insights, connections and opportunities do you have to share. Remember, their lives are fraught with issues and challenges, too.

-65-
Tend To Relationships

In his book *The Culture Solution*, motivational speaker and business consultant Matthew Kelly shares, "Life and business falls into a tyranny of urgent, which demands we rush from one urgent thing to the next. The problem is that building relationships is hardly urgent, but it is important."

As Kelly implies, while we need to tend to the fires in our personal and professional lives, we also need to have the presence of mind to stop from time to time, take a deep breath and pull back from those intense moments. And then, in that pause, reach out and reconnect with the important people around us. Our families. Our neighbors. Our colleagues. Employees. Vendors. And even those we encounter that don't fall under any of those headings.

Yes, the crisis of the moment just might be part of the modern world. But relationships have and forever will be the most important part of life. Tend to them often.

-66-
Nobly Agree to Disagree

According to the book *Foundational Networking: Building Know, Like and Trust To Create A Lifetime of Extraordinary Success*, "if you meet someone with a differing opinion, agree to disagree. Don't just press your point."

You live in a wonderful country. It's vast in geography. It plays host to dozens of cultures. It is a melting pot of nationalities, races and religions. It has a broad spectrum of political and ideological views. And it allows for the freedom to express most any perspective.

With all of that, you shouldn't be surprised that others have thoughts that don't align with yours. What of it? You might be surprised that it doesn't happen more often.

Remember, you might not always agree with other people's thoughts, ideas, and perspective. That, however, doesn't stop you from doing the heavy lifting of seeking commonalities, strengthening what you do agree on, and remaining mindful of the person's feelings. This is what makes agreeing to disagree an act of nobility.

-67-
Network Anywhere; Network Everywhere

When someone mentions networking, your mind may immediately conjure up images of the latest business after-hours or a corporate golf outing. But the act of connecting with others is not limited to things officially dubbed as "networking events."

When you volunteer your time with a charitable organization, you're networking. The same is true if you lend your expertise to a civic organization or school initiative.

You don't need a special invitation to embark on networking. You create it by your very action. Giving a referral is networking. So is sharing information or making an introduction.

You're networking if you do something as simple as being complimentary towards another. The same is true if you are encouraging or empathetic.

The reality is that you can network virtually anywhere and opportunities to network are everywhere. So to build your network all you need is the desire to interact with others and the initiative to do so.

-68-
The Four Pillars

In his book *MORE: Word of Mouth Referrals, Lifelong Customers and Raving Fans*, professional speaker Matt Ward shares what he refers to as The Four Pillars of caring for people in your network. These are:

One, over-deliver. In demonstrating the notion of caring, it's imperative for you to find ways to ensure that you are not just meeting other's expectations, but consistently and substantially exceeding them.

Two, listen. As Ward asserts, caring involves both listening and looking for information someone shares that alerts you to how you can help them.

Three, surprise. Your acts of caring should come out of nowhere. It should be something that completely marvels someone in a wonderful way. And,

Four, non-self-serving. When you execute a caring act, you need to remove all reference to your professional interests, which could include refraining from using a business card or any marketing material.

Use these four pillars to care for those you know, and your network will support you in return.

-69-
Steal A March

"Steal a March" is a metaphoric expression that has its roots in medieval warfare. Back in that time, a march was simply the distance an army could travel in a day. And if one army could get in a day's travel that its opponent could not, they were said to have stolen a march. So, to steal a march is to gain an unexpected or secret advantage over a rival.

But you don't need to focus on a competitor to steal a march. If you innovate on how you get things done, you've stolen a march on your current process. If you put in a little extra effort each and every day, you've stolen a march over the status quo. And if you double down for a time to build great strategic partnerships, you've stolen a march on the lackluster network you currently have.

So, ponder the question, "How can I steal a march over where I am today?"

-70-
Mimic Great Behavior

The key to successful networking is getting lots of great people knowing you. This, raises the question, "What do I want people to know about me?"

The best way to answer that is to ask yourself, "What do I want to know about other people?"

Certainly, you want to know that they are action oriented. So, conduct yourself so that is the persona that others see.

You also want to know that someone has a degree of selflessness, sharing with the world around them. Knowing that, you need to double down on being that person too.

And, of course, you want to know that someone is reliable and trustworthy, as you have a natural trust for those who do what they say they are going to do. With that, you should become a person upon whom others can rely.

In short, you should try to mimic the behaviors you look for in others. *Become the person you want to associate with.*

-71-
Opening Relationships

On his blog, *The Sales Hunter*, Mark Hunter shares, "We don't close sales with customers, we open relationships to create the next sale. Your customers are not bowling pins waiting to be knocked over, they are customers waiting for you to open a relationship with. Too many salespeople see customers as nothing more than a barrier they need to blow through to earn their commission. This is the reason why I do not like the term 'closing' a sale. I prefer to say we are 'opening' a relationship."

Hunter makes a great distinction. A sale is a one-time transaction. At best, it goes well. And even if it does, that's it. You're left looking for the next deal.

A relationship, however, is different. It's almost a living, breathing being that offers ongoing benefits in both directions.

Here's the thing: Whether you close sales or open relationships is entirely up to you. It's a mindset and a commitment to act on that attitude.

-72-
Statements Versus Questions

In an interview on the full *Networking Rx* podcast, communication researcher and Denison University Associate Professor Dr. Laura Russell made the point that when we make statements, we push our thoughts and views on others. However, when we ask questions, we invite others to share what they know and believe.

She goes on to explain that as humans we have an almost universal 'need to be needed.' And so, by asking questions, we invite others to demonstrate their value. And when they have an opportunity to answer, they gain the sense they're needed.

Dr. Russell challenges herself to be mindful of the ratio of 'statements she makes' to 'questions she asks.' She does this when communicating with her colleagues, her students and generally anyone she has a conversation with. While there is no target ratio, being aware helps her to ask more questions. And in so doing, she allows others to share more value.

The beautiful thing is that this is a challenge you can easily adopt.

-73-
The Need For Networking

Just like getting in shape, networking is not something you embark upon only when you need a job or want to make a sale. Rather, it is an ongoing process that has no real beginning and certainly no end.

You may be perfectly content with your professional existence. However, outside forces can change that fast. And even if that doesn't happen, your internal drives will push you to advance beyond where you are. An ongoing regime of building professional relationships with those around you will position you for that unforeseen event or desired personal growth.

You may currently have a full plate of customers or clients. Great. However, nothing lasts forever. Projects end. The need for what you offer diminishes. Competition cuts into your book of business. In short, to remain busy, you have an enduring need to network.

In summary, to continue to enjoy success at any level, your need for networking is continual.

-74-
Why You Don't Get What You Want

According to Michael Maher, author of the popular book *The Seven Levels of Communication: Go From Relationships to Referrals*, "the reason why people don't get the business that they want, is because they are too focused on getting the business they want." While Maher's comment is cute, it's very insightful, as well as very indicting of some people.

Your brain is capable of amazing feats of intellect. However, your conscious mind can't focus on more than one thing at a time. So, when you're always focused on trying to get business, you're impaired from helping others. And thus, you won't be building relationships. And without relationships, you'll never get referrals. And without referrals, you'll struggle to get all the business that you want.

So, if Maher's insight is true, so is the reverse: If you help others get the business they want, you'll get the business you want.

-75-
Spread Love

One of the many quotes from Saint Teresa of Calcutta, better known as Mother Teresa, is "Spread love wherever you go. Let no one ever come to you without leaving happier." We tend to think of love as being akin to deep, romantic affection, but Mother Teresa's heartwarming thought reminds us that the concept of love is much broader than that.

Think about it. At this moment, you have the power to do a little something extra for someone else. You can offer a kind word. You can make them smile, maybe even laugh. You can warm someone's soul with a friendly deed, such as holding a door open, giving up a seat for another or simply lending a sympathetic ear.

This list could go on and on. And none of it diminishes you financially or devalues your standing in life. But any of it ... any tiny bit of it ... serves to leave another happier.

You truly have the power to spread love.

-76-
Four Simple Realities

Here are four simple realities. The first is that in life, you've accomplished nothing alone. It's true. Every feat or achievement has involved the help of others. So, you need others to move you along.

The second simple reality is that much of what you need, others are not aware of. They aren't, as what's in your head and heart is invisible to them. So, if you need something, you need to ask.

The third simple reality is that others want to help you – they really do. The human existence is hardwired with the need to help others. So, don't be afraid to ask for help.

And the final simple reality ... and it's the most beautiful reality ... is that if you ask others for help, and do it in a positive, polite manner, they are not only likely to help you, but they'll be flattered you saw enough value in them to ask. This will create in their mind a positive impression about you.

-77-
Me Versus Me

In his book *No One Gets There Alone*, elite performance psychologist Dr. Rob Bell shares that we're all athletes. Some athletic. Some corporate. Some entrepreneurial. But we're all athletes.

With that, he makes the point that the best athletes know their toughest competition is against themselves and that's not easy, but it is the most rewarding. Competing with yourself is about challenging yourself to become the best you can.

Bell shares, "It becomes a competition against ourselves if we refuse that piece of cake or get that workout in or wake up when our alarm goes off or help out someone else."

He implies that this self-competition is a mindset where you know and strive to get better, every day, in every way. You, in essence, focus on being the best at getting better.

Sure, there are those who want the same job you do and others who look to lure your clients away, but as Bell reminds, "True competition is me versus me."

-78-
The Around the World Walk-On

In 2012, Brian Rice was just like any other freshman playing basketball in the NCAA Division III. No scholarship. School before sports. Playing before small crowds. The Geneva College freshman was just like any other college basketball player, except for one thing. He was 43 years old.

You see, Rice always dreamed of playing college basketball. And when he was a senior in high school, there were colleges ready to utilize his basketball talents at the next level. But Rice was not ready for college.

So rather than college, he opted for a short stint in the Navy. Little did Rice know, however, that the short stint would turn into almost 25 years travelling the world, serving his country in both war and peace. But his dream to play college basketball never died and so he saw it through.

The lesson is that it's never too late to chase a dream or embark on something new.

-79-
Tips For Improving Small Talk

"Small Talk" is a skill and here are some ideas for becoming more proficient at it.

First, think. On the way to the next event or when you have some idle time, work through in your mind how you envision your "small talk" going. Review the questions you will ask in your mind. See yourself listening, summarizing, and sharing.

Second, listen. "Small talk" is all around you, every day. Listen to it, especially those who are good at it. See how they weave from one question to the next and how they transition to business, return to small talk and then exit the conversation.

Finally, engage. Take every opportunity to engage in "small talk". When you are in line at the store checkout. With a server in a restaurant. With the receptionist at your next appointment. You will find the more you engage in small talk, the better you get at it.

Small talk is a skill. Commit to improving it.

-80-
The World Is a Mirror

In the opening pages of her book, *The 11 Laws of Likability*, Michelle Lederman relates an experience where her father was attempting to explain to her his long-standing mantra, "The World Is A Mirror."

Lederman shares, "Then one day he stood me in front of a mirror and said, 'Smile.' I did, and the person in the mirror smiled back at me. He said, 'Look angry.' I gave the girl in the mirror a nasty look and got the same nasty look right back. He then sat me down and explained the lesson: What you show the world is what the world will show you."

The lesson that Lederman's father gave her is now yours. But the lesson begs the question: What do you intend to show the world today? A smile or a grimace? Will you project enthusiasm or lethargy? Optimism or pessimism?

Whatever you want from the world, you first need to put out into it.

-81-
Create Hope

Years ago, a group of researchers conducted a study. They would place a rat in a glass container of water, far too deep to touch the bottom and with no means of escape. Then the researchers would turn out all the lights. In total darkness, the rat would drown in a matter of minutes.

Then they would place another rat in a similar container of water and leave the lights on. That rat would tread water for hours and hours.

Why the difference? The ability to see gave the second rat hope. The lesson is that hope is a powerful thing, and not just for rats. Humans thrive on it as well.

Whenever you fall on hard times, find a means of creating hope. Somehow take a small step in a positive direction, so that you can see a way forward. Know that just a little bit of hope will drive you to keep going and going. Do whatever you can to create hope.

-82-
Say Cheese

What is the quickest, easiest, and most effective thing you can do to improve your rapport with friends and strangers? The answer is simple: Smile.

It's true. Smiling is super easy. Actually, it's natural. And it's lightning fast. Study after study shows that you can greatly enhance how you are perceived and how you affect the world around you by making an effort to have a genuine grin on your face.

Why? Well, perhaps it's just common sense, but the reality is that people want to associate with those who make them feel good. And when you carry a smile, research shows that other people naturally smile back.

And the act of smiling causes the human body to release feel good hormones. So, when you help another person smile, they naturally feel good and they associate that feeling with you.

So, say cheese in a genuine way. And in so doing build your network as you brighten the lives of others.

-83-
Share Yourself

Leadership and executive communication expert, John Millen shared on his *Sunday Coffee* blog "Giving people a glimpse of who you are, builds trust because before we can trust people, we must get to know them."

Millen goes on to share that many leaders feel uncomfortable sharing themselves or can't decide how to break the wall between their personal and business lives. He then offers advice for circumventing this.

He writes, "The best way to share yourself is to tell your story. As humans, we are hard-wired for storytelling, which is why we become so engaged when we hear stories. Risk vulnerability by sharing yourself and your story. Give them insight into what you're doing, especially your interactions with noteworthy employees, clients and others."

While Millen works with executives of major corporations, his advice has value, no matter who or what you might lead. Share your story. Share yourself. Give them a glimpse of you. This will fortify you with the trust of others.

-84-
Fix Your Network

In essence, your network is just a service business. Think about it. You offer value to others based on their needs. Then, in return you receive the value you need.

As such, just like any other service-based business, an important part of growing and maintaining your network is marketing it to others. That is, somehow communicating the value you have to offer.

In his book *Selling the Invisible,* author Harry Beckwith shares that the first step to effectively marketing any service is to fix it. After all, it makes little sense to communicate about a service that has flaws, right?

To do this, Beckwith encourages you to take a constructive, but critical look at yourself. Assume that things are not perfect. Be honest. What do you see? What could you improve? Make a list.

Then with that list in hand, commit to quietly fix the issues. This exercise will improve you and at the same time give you a better network to offer.

-85-
Spice Up Your Introduction

Having an effective means of introducing yourself is good, and important. But not relying on just one introduction is even better.

To make this happen, consider developing a variety of message bodies. Make some informative or educational, others flippant or amusing, and still others something with a little shock value (to really grab someone's attention).

You might also vary the reason "why" people should refer you. What information about you or your company will instill confidence and boost your credibility? What sets you apart?

Another option is to vary who you seek. In some settings you can outright ask people to refer you clients. In others, ask for a connection to a strategic partner. Or maybe you need to ask for information (such as details on networking events, job transition groups or backgrounds on people).

It does not matter how you slice or dice the framework. The key is to come with various ways to spice up your introduction.

-86-
The Blessings Exercise

In a newsletter entitled *Positive Psychology Tools with the Biggest Bang for Your Buck,* executive coach and relationship expert Dr. John Schinnerer shared that an effective way of improving you overall happiness is the "blessings exercise."

Schinnerer encourages "Every three to five nights, write down three things that went well that day and why they went well."

He goes on to elaborate that the exercise is a very simple yet powerful way to begin to shift your thinking. You'll go from being focused on what you lack to being focused on what you have. And in as few as a couple of committed weeks, you'll pull yourself out of a depression or create a heightened degree of optimism.

So today, and a couple more times over the next week, look at your life. What are the things that went well? Note them. Then dig a little deeper to uncover why they went well. In time, you'll find your life is truly a blessing.

-87-
Creativity Is Contagious

Albert Einstein, a physicist who developed the theory of relativity, one of the two pillars of modern physics, once remarked, "Creativity is contagious. Pass it on."

Think about Einstein's quote. Ideas tend to build on one another over time. For example, a small flame in a caveman's hand rolled forward over the eons and eventually served to launch a man onto the moon.

Whether you realize it or not, you are part of this process. Today, you are capitalizing on the creativity and innovation of others. You rely on the electricity of Franklin, Tesla and Edison. You utilize computers and software innovation. The Internet. Wifi. Spreadsheets. Word processors. And the like.

You are in this moment with a litany of tools brought forth by the creativity of others. Use those tools to revolutionize how your world operates, even if just in some small way. Others will capitalize on that. And then serve to make it better. And just like that your moment of creativity has infected others in a wonderful way.

-88-
Be A Hero

Everyone loves a hero. Everyone adores the notion of Superman flying in to save the day, with no time to spare. Everyone admires doctors, nurses and first responders of every type, who selflessly put others above themselves. Everyone marvels at the person who becomes immersed in that "cause" that serves to better the entire community.

Yes, everyone loves a hero. Knowing this, commit to becoming a hero for someone today. It can be as easy as giving referrals that serve to make someone's day, month, or year. Or making introductions to key strategic partners. It might be simply sharing useful information or unique opportunities with those who need them most.

The more you can do for people in your world, the more you become a hero. And the more you do for your world, the more your world will do for you. So, who will you be a hero for today?

-89-
Do Your Homework

On her popular *Networking Ninja* YouTube series, body language expert Alison Henderson encourages you to do your homework before venturing out to network. Your homework consists of three things.

First, find out who's going to be there. If possible, check who has RSVPed for the event. Based on what you learn, determine who you'd like to meet or the particular industry or business sector you'd like to focus on.

Next, prior to the event, try to make contact with a few of the people you'd like to meet. Then seek them out once you arrive.

Finally, know the dress code for the event. This will allow you to show up and be the best possible representative of your company or personal brand.

Henderson's point is that doing your homework on the front end will help you get more out of the event once you arrive.

-90-
Beyond Recognition

If you want your network to connect you to referrals, they first need to know, like and trust you. Additionally, you need to educate them on how to recognize what a good referral looks like.

Those two things, however, are not enough. You also need to empower your network with the ability to talk to prospective clients about what it is you do.

For example, an auto insurance agent first needs to get her referral partners to recognize that someone with a teenage driver could be a good opportunity. But she also needs to educate those partners on how to work into a conversation with such a person a question like, "What has having a teen driver done to your insurance premiums?"

This brings insurance into the conversation. And, in time, allows the referral partner to suggest that the prospect might consult with the auto insurance agent. No, this doesn't guarantee a new client, but it gets the situation beyond simple recognition of a potential opportunity.

-91-
Create Triads

In the book *Tribal Leadership*, the authors encourage the creation of triads. Essentially, a triad is when one person connects two people who previously didn't know each other. Simple, right?

The authors acknowledge that while there is nothing wrong with being the go-between for two individuals, it can be time consuming and is not scalable.

That said, triads have great potential. Think about it. You know lots of people. But not all those people know each other. This creates an amazing opportunity for you to serve.

You serve to expand the network of two people you know. And at the same time, you serve to build your personal brand as a connector. Best of all, it's simple. It's effective. And it's powerful.

So, what triad are you going to create today? More importantly, how are you going to share the notion of triads with others and inspire them to start building them too? This might lead to something wonderful for you.

-92-
Extending Your Gratitude

There are times each year where we naturally pause to express appreciation for all that the universe and the people around us have done to enrich our lives. Thanksgiving and Christmas come to mind.

However, Kristen Schmitt, leadership coach and founder of Thrive to Lead, ponders on her blog: "What if we were to expand that practice and quieted our inner critics for a time? We could take a moment to acknowledge and appreciate ourselves for all that we do for others. Caring for our loved ones. Being a (mainly) good parent. Going above and beyond at work. Mentoring others. Extending kindness to strangers."

Schmitt is right. The tradition of giving thanks is a wonderful one. It's more than wonderful. It's beautiful. Work to make it an everyday thing. Or at least something more than a once or twice a year thing.

-93-
Be the Modest Winner

Do you know what the world doesn't appreciate? A sore loser. You know, the person who displays a miserable disposition in the face of a setback. So, don't be a poor sport about things.

Do you know what the world appreciates even less than the sore loser? The person who excessively celebrates and gloats when things go their way. Don't be this person either.

Remember that the world respects a modest winner as much as it does the loser who demonstrates great sportsmanship. So when things go your way – you know, when you land that great client, get the big promotion, or your team scores that award – you're best to carry an air of humility no matter how well things are going.

Yes, be proud of yourself relative to whatever you achieve and know that others will likely be impressed by your accomplishments., However, when you remain as grounded in victory as in defeat, others will also appreciate the humble nature with which you achieve them.

-94-
The Never-Ending Job

As a businessperson, you need things today. Things like referrals, information, and contacts. Guess what? You are going to need those things tomorrow, and the next day, and next year. Thus, creating and nurturing productive relationships is an ongoing endeavor. Your job is never done.

Know this: Some days your networking efforts are going to seem worthwhile. It is easy to keep after it. Other days your networking efforts are going to seem like a complete waste. You will want to swear it off. Don't.

You need to have faith. Opportunity comes from the most unlikely places. And opportunity tends to surface when you least expect it. But it's all the result of productive relationships.

So, never quit trying to build relationships in your life. Continually strive to get others to know you, like you, and trust you. And to make that happen you need to consistently strive to be generous, caring and committed towards others. And this job is never done.

-95-
Zero Talent

Recently on Twitter, Steve Gutzler, consultant and author of *Emotional Intelligence for Personal Leadership,* shared a reminder that there are eight things that require zero talent:

1) Being on time
2) Personal drive
3) High energy
4) Being passionate
5) Having a positive attitude
6) Strong body language
7) Doing extra
8) Praising others

No, there is nothing groundbreaking about Gutzler's reminder. But isn't that the point? You can take action on each and every one of these items today...right now. Get after your day so you're on time, and in so doing you exhibit high energy and personal drive. Stand tall and wear a genuine smile and you cannot help but exude passion and a positive attitude. And then go out of your way to praise someone in a way that completely flatters them and makes their day.

And all the things on this list will serve to brand you in a positive way.

-96-
Relationship, Relationship, Relationship

In the world of successful brick-and-mortar business the three most important things are location, location, and location. When it comes to building a network of great people in your life, however, location really doesn't matter at all.

In reality, if you want to create a strong, vibrant network where you can both share and reap the benefits of great referrals, new contacts, unique opportunities and useful information, the three most important things are relationship, relationship, and relationship.

It's true. In building a productive network, where you're located is of little importance. And do you know what matter even less? The style of clothes you wear. The car you drive. They type of office furniture. Or whether or not you belong to a country club.

The only thing that matters in your network are the relationships. That's it. Given that fact, you need to double down on adding value to others. Share referrals. Make introductions. Enlighten others to unique opportunities and useful information. From that, your network will build.

-97-
The Benefits of Social Media

Social media is not a replacement for networking. It is, however, a great a tool to help you network. Used properly, it can help you in one of three ways.

First, social media is an effective means of networking through to people. In short, social media is a great way to find and work through strategic partners who can lead you to clients.

Second, social media provides you a platform to brand yourself as a knowledgeable and committed person in your profession (someone to know, like and trust). It won't happen overnight, but in time you can be considered the expert.

Finally, social media is a great means of finding opportunity. You can use it to find events that can lead you to clients. You can get information that can connect you to clients. And prospective clients can become aware of you and connect with you directly.

Using social media will not create an immediate windfall. Over time, however, the benefits will accrue.

-98-
Better Than Gold

In her book *The Empathy Edge: Harnessing the Value of Compassion as an Engine for Success,* corporate branding expert Maria Ross shares:

"We often think of empathy as the Golden Rule: *do unto others as you would have done unto you.* But here's the problem: Not everyone thinks or feels the way you do. A better way to act with empathy is to follow what has become known as the Platinum Rule: *Treat others as they want to be treated.*"

As Ross implies, stepping into the shoes of another, seeing and feeling the world from their perspective, and then acting on that is better than what society has come to know as the "gold standard" for treating others.

This Platinum Rule forces you to see things from the other person's point of view. And by doing that, whatever action you undertake is likely to have a more positive impact on the person you've devoted attention to. Platinum is truly better than gold.

-99-
Double Down On This

Yes. Absolutely. By all means, be generous to the world around you. Add value in your own way, or any way you can. Give referrals. Make introductions. Share ideas and information. Be empathetic. Be encouraging.

But know this: People will accept your contributions in one of four ways.

One. They might do nothing. Failing to acknowledge your efforts at all. Oh well. You weren't looking for something anyway.

Two. They might take the time to thank you. And that's nice. It's good to be appreciated.

Three. Some might say thanks, but then offer up other ways you can serve them. Steer clear of this trap.

And finally, some will thank you, and then endeavor to match the value you've shared by offering to share with you the value they have to offer.

Pay attention to this fourth group. Double down on your efforts to serve it. These are the people to invest effort in, as that effort is sure to yield a handsome return.

-100-
Deadlines Drive Results

In this fast-paced world with lots of things competing for your time and attention, you likely find yourself moving to complete things very close to the time they are absolutely due. Think about it.

Most tax returns get filed on April 15th. And college term papers are generally only completed within hours of being due. People tend to put their trash out for pick up when they hear the garbage truck lumbering down the street.

This is true of anything. Even in your professional life. If you give yourself 30 days to outline the book you contemplate writing, it will take you 30 days. If you give yourself an hour, you'll get it done in 60 minutes.

Remember, deadlines drive results. Knowing this, create some urgency in your life. Give yourself deadlines and attach some importance to meeting those targets. You will procrastinate less. And you will get more done.

-101-
Fall In Love With No

Nobody likes rejection. It simply hurts to get that clear indication that you're not getting a new client ... or not getting hired ... or not getting promoted. So, no one likes to hear the word, 'NO.'

Of course, you'd rather hear 'YES.' Something like, "You're the person. We need you," lights up your world.

But 'NO' is a wonderful thing. Sure, it's disappointing. But with that one simple word, there is closure. And you can move forward. And that's a whole lot better than never hearing back. Or being strung along with what feels like a never-ending cycle of "We're still thinking about it."

Rejection is not ideal. But it is liberating. You can learn from it. And move forward and be better equipped for the next experience. So, fall in love with the word 'NO.' It will help you get to 'YES."

There you have it—101 essays. But we wanted to offer a bonus essay. Before we do, if you're interested in exploring other books, content, and programs by Frank Agin, visit frankagin.com or simply search "Frank Agin" on whatever platform you use to get great content.

-102-
Surefire Network Jump-Start

It's a common dilemma: You neither have the personality nor the interested in schmoozing at area networking events. And yet, at the same time, your network is not what you want it to be, and you feel the need to re-invigorate it.

So, you're looking for a quick, surefire means of bolstering your network. The answer to this dilemma is simple. Determine what you're passionate about and find somewhere to volunteer.

Yes, volunteer. You see, volunteerism will help network you in two ways. First, when you serve whatever your passionate about, you don't do so alone. Rather, you'll be shoulder to shoulder with a plethora of new contacts who share your interest.

Second, others see you giving back to the community. And because of that, they are drawn to you and want to associate with you – even if they don't share your passion for something. So, find what ignites your soul, and get out and volunteer.

About The Author

Frank Agin is president of AmSpirit Business Connections, which empowers entrepreneurs, sales representatives, and professionals to become successful and gain more referrals through networking.

He also shares information and insights on professional relationships, business networking and best practices for generating referrals on his Networking Rx podcast and through various professional programs.

Finally, Frank is the author of several books, including *Foundational Networking: Building Know, Like & Trust to Create a Life of Extraordinary Success*. See all his books and programs at frankagin.com. You can reach him at frankagin@amspirit.com.